W9-DHU-404

NAVAJO NATIVE DYES
Their Preparation and Use

NONABAH G. BRYAN
AND STELLA YOUNG

DOVER PUBLICATIONS, INC.
Mineola, New York

Published in Canada by General Publishing Company, Ltd., 895 Don Mills Road, 400-2 Park Centre, Toronto, Ontario M3C 1W3.

Published in the United Kingdom by David & Charles, Brunel House, Forde Close, Newton Abbot, Devon TQ12 4PU.

Bibliographical Note

This Dover edition, first published in 2002, is an unabridged republication of the text and illustrations of the work originally published in 1940 by the Education Division of the U.S. Office of Indian Affairs, the U.S. Department of the Interior, Washington, D.C.

Library of Congress Cataloging-in-Publication Data

Young, Stella.
     Navajo native dyes : their preparation and use / [recipes formulated by] Nonabah G. Bryan ; and [compiled by] Stella Young.
          p. cm.
     Originally published: Chilocco, Okla. : Printing Dept., Chilocco Agricultural School, [1940] in series: Indian handcrafts ; 2.
     ISBN 0-486-42105-8 (pbk.)
     1. Navajo textile fabrics. 2. Dyes and dyeing—Southwest, New. 3. Navajo Indians—Industries. 4. Dye plants—Southwest, New. I. Bryan, Nonabah Gorman. II. Title.

E99.N3 Y7 2002
666'.26'089972—dc21

                                                                                      2002018819

Manufactured in the United States of America
Dover Publications, Inc., 31 East 2nd Street, Mineola, N.Y. 11501

Contents

Introduction

With the introduction of sheep into the Southwest by the Spaniards in the latter half of the sixteenth century, wool became a fiber accessible to the Navajo people. Contact with the Pueblo Indians introduced them to the upright loom. Navajo genius discovered that the plants and minerals of their desert home could be used to change the native white and black wool to a multitude of soft and lustrous colors. Blended on the upright loom, these produced the antique Navajo rugs so much prized for their simplicity in design, which consists for the most part of variations of simple stripes, and for their colors—the pale yellows, browns, grays, tans, and rose, which reflect the beauty of the desert.

Recognizing the unique achievements of these ancient art-craftspeople and desiring to perpetuate their art, the Home Economics Department at the Wingate Vocational High School undertook in 1934 to revive interest in native dyed rugs by discovering how these native dyes were obtained. This bulletin is a record of the research and experimentation carried on in the course of the study.

The department was fortunate in having on its staff Mrs. Nonabah G. Bryan, a Navajo woman, educated in government schools, and familiar with the reservation, having spent most of her life on it. She was employed to teach Navajo weaving, at which she has become an artist. Much of her effort during the past few years has been spent in perfecting native dyes. She has used in the process only those materials procurable from the reservation. Her foundation recipes are largely those of her ancestors—making of black dye by mixing the mineral yellow ocher with pitch from the piñon (*Pinus edulis*) and dye water from the three-leaved sumac (*Rhus trilobata*); and obtaining yellows and browns by the boiling of certain plants with raw alum or water from juniper ashes (*Juniperus monosperma*). But the dyeing of rose yarn by fermenting prickly pear cactus fruit (*Opuntia polycantha*), and the making of green by first dyeing the yarn yellow with sagebrush (*Artemisia tridentata*) and later putting it in a black afterbath dye water, are her own discoveries.

At the beginning of the study only standard plants were used, but as the work progressed, a wide variety were utilized in the hope that Indians from all parts of the reservation could find satisfactory products close enough to their homes to make this method of dyeing practicable. Many new shades and tints have been developed through experimentation with different plant combinations as well as by varying the recipes used for dyeing with the same plant.

The yellows are the easiest of all to obtain and range from clear yellow through green yellows to mustard. The browns may be light or dark and often have considerable red, rose, or purple in them. The black made from the mineral ocher, pitch from the piñon (*Pinus edulis*), and the three-leaved sumac (*Rhus trilobata*), is bluish-black and is quite different from the brown-black of the natural black sheep. Tans, grays, orange, pinks, and rose appear frequently in native dyed rugs. A good green was never obtained in ancient times from strictly reservation materials. The yarn was first dyed yellow and then boiled in indigo blue to make the desired shade or tint of green. Indigo was obtained by the Indians through trade with Mexico. Some very yellow greens have been made from plants grown locally. The Denver Museum of Art, Indian Leaflet Series No. 74, states that the bark and berries of the one-seeded juniper (*Juniperus monosperma*) are used for dyeing wool green; in the Fort Wingate experiments, however, the bast and sprigs of the one-seeded juniper have yielded only an orange-tan and a yellow-tan (page 34 of the present publication). In 1936 Mrs. Bryan discovered an interesting process for making green by dyeing yarn yellow with sagebrush (*Artemisia tridentata*), or orange with Navajo tea (*Thelesperma gracile*), and then boiling this in the afterbath dye water from native black dye (pages 53 and 58). By this method a number of interesting shades and tints can be obtained. These native dyes were combined with cream, gray, brown, and brown-black of the natural wool.

The old Navajo had no exact measurements and even today on the reservation only approximate measures are used. Cactus fruit, plants, and the barks of various trees are measured in pans, sumac and Navajo tea are made into rolls, and rugs are so many hand-lengths in size. Sufficient supplies of either wool or dye materials were seldom on hand so they used what they had. If, in the early spring, the supply of wool was depleted, a strip a few inches wide was sheared along either side of the backbone of the sheep. More could not be taken lest the animal die of cold. For these reasons every rug was an experiment. If there was an insufficiency of warp or woof yarn for a large rug a small one was made instead and the design modified to fit it. If the supply of mountain mahogany root bark ran out, ground lichens might be substituted or several plants mixed together to approximate the desired color. A rug had to be made to be traded for necessary food.

As the Navajo of today is trained to accumulate supplies for a year in advance, planned rugs may now be woven. The weaver will continue to create the design and work out the color scheme for the individual rug as in time past. Exactitude in the making of rugs is now a possibility and the weaver need not be curtailed in the accomplishment of her dream by the necessity of substituting what she has for what she would like to have.

It is now becoming possible to use exact recipes for dyes on the reservation. It has been the purpose of the Home Economics Department of the Wingate Vocational High School to assist in discovering methods that are practical and in formulating recipes for dyes made entirely from reservation products. Those so formulated up to March 1935 were published at that time in a mimeographed bulletin by the school. This new publication also includes those which have been developed since then.

A number of books have already been written on this subject. The justification for this present publication lies in the fact that it contains definitely formulated recipes, and that recipes developed through our own experimentation are included.

Working with Mrs. Bryan through this series of experiments has been a pleasant and profitable experience.

Grateful acknowledgment is given to the following people for their generous help during the preparation of this bulletin. To Mr. Herman Bogard, Superintendent of the Wingate Vocational High School, and to Mr. Leroy F. Jackson, former Superintendent of the school, for their generous cooperation which has made this study possible; to Dr. Ruth Underhill, Associate Supervisor of Indian Education (Anthropologist), for assistance in editing the bulletin; to Dr. E. F. Castetter, Professor of Botany and to Mr. Francis H. Elmore, of the University of New Mexico for the botanical classification of the dye plants; to Dr. John D. Clark, Professor of Chemistry at the University of New Mexico, for the chemical analysis and classification of the rocks used; to Father Berard Haile of Gallup, and to Dr. John P. Harrington of the Smithsonian Institution, for the Navajo names for the plants and minerals used; to Mr. Charles Keetsie Shirley, illustrator for the Navajo Service, for the drawings of the dye plants; and to all others who have in any way contributed to the experimental study or to the writing of the bulletin.

STELLA YOUNG

Ft. Wingate, New Mexico, 1939.
Wingate Vocational High School

Mrs. Bryan Dyes Yarn
for a Rug

Mrs. Bryan decides to dye some yarns for a native-dye rug. She plans to use a brown made from mountain mahogany root bark (*Cercocarpus montanus*), rose from prickly-pear-cactus fruit (*Opunta polycantha*), green from sagebrush (*Artemisia tridentata*) and black afterbath dye water, black from ocher, piñon pitch (*Pinus edulis*) and three-leaved sumac (*Rhus trilobata*), and white from cream-colored wool whitened with gypsum.

From her store of supplies she selects the materials, which she has gathered one by one at the proper season during the past year. From the mountains she has dug mountain mahogany roots in the early fall, at which time they give the strongest color. As soon as they were dug she pounded the bark from them and dried it. The last of September she traveled to the nearest mesa, where she knew from experience a bed of prickly pear grew. She picked the red fruit, rubbed it in the sand to remove the thorns, and carried it home and dried it. She went twenty-five miles to a coal mine, where she gathered her year's supply of ocher. Having found it at this place the year before, she was quite sure she could do it again. She knew a spot in the foothills of the mountains where there was a great deal of pitch on the piñon trees. She gathered cans full of it one day as she passed the place on her way home from a squaw dance. She took down several rolls of dried sumac, which she had gathered the summer before from the arroyo at the back of the Wingate school. Sagebrush was no problem because it grew all around her, stayed green all winter, and only required picking. She gathered the whitener, gypsum, where she had found it many times before in some shale near a coal deposit.

As she checked over her supplies the only things she lacked were her mordants. The raw alum was in a can where it had been placed as she gathered it from under certain large rocks found in the flat reservation country. The one-seeded juniper (*Juniperus monosperma*) twigs she gathers fresh from the foothills of the mountains just back of her home the evening before she needs them.

She has been carding and spinning her warp and woof yarns for several weeks. Her wool has been shorn from sheep which produce a high-quality blanket wool. For this reason it has not been necessary for her to wash it before carding, because it contains little grease and picks up a minimum of dirt. She has, however, shaken it well and spread it on the sand, shorn side up, and sprinkled it with white clay which she had previously gathered in certain arid regions in the Navajo country. As the sun heats the grease, the clay absorbs it. After shaking it again thoroughly, she cards it. Once she has her yarn spun she washes it before she dyes it.

She takes from her supplies some soapweed (*Yucca baccata*) which she dug one day while out on the mesa. She had already crushed the root, heated it over hot coals and dried it so that it would keep indefinitely. Now that she is ready to use it she rubs some of it in cold water until there is a heavy lather. Before beginning, she is careful to free her hands and the tub of oil or grease; otherwise, the root would produce no lather. After removing the soapweed, she adds hot water to make it comfortably warm for washing. She sudses the yarn up and down, but is careful not to rub or twist it, because she doesn't want it to get lumpy. When it is clean, she rinses it thoroughly and hangs it up to dry.

With yarn clean and dye materials assembled, she is ready to do the actual dyeing. The rose yarn is dyed first, because it takes a week or sometimes two to complete the process. She selects an enamel kettle for dyeing, because she has found that if she does it in tin or aluminum the acid developed in the dyebath while it is fermenting reacts upon the metal, and the color of the dye is changed. She measures out the dried prickly-pear fruit and covers it with lukewarm water to soak overnight. In the morning she mashes it well, strains it, and adds enough more cool water to cover the yarn completely. She then places the wet yarn in it, rubs the dye into it well, covers it, and sets it in a warm place to ferment, having learned from previous experience that if she boils it, the lovely rose color will change to tan. Many times each day during the following week she rubs the dye into the yarn. If she finds at the end of the time that the rose color is not as deep as she wishes it, she puts it in another dyebath of the same strength as before and allows it to ferment another week. She then rinses it thoroughly and hangs it up to dry.

The black yarn, which she dyes next, is the most difficult of all to prepare. She first puts the sumac on to boil. Then she grinds the chunks of ocher between Navajo grinding stones to a fine powder and toasts it to cocoa brown in a frying pan, after which she adds the piñon pitch, a little at a time, stirring it constantly. It smokes and makes her eyes, throat, and nose smart, but she continues to stir it until this smoke has all passed off. During this heating process, the pitch has reduced the iron in the ocher to a ferrous compound. She lets it cool until just lukewarm and then adds it to the sumac dyebath water which she has previously strained from the twigs. The tannin in the sumac water unites with the ferrous compound in the ocher-and-pitch mixture and makes black ink. She stirs the dyebath well and notes that there is a sufficient quantity so the yarn can float in it. She lets it boil a few minutes, then adds the wet yarn. She prefers to use the natural black yarn, as it dyes black more easily. She stirs this well as she desires to distribute the dye evenly into all parts of the wool. After it has boiled for two or three hours, she takes the kettle from the stove and leaves the yarn in the dyebath overnight, because she thinks this makes a faster dye. In the morning she rinses it two or three times, or until the color ceases to run out into the water, and hangs it up to dry.

She plans to do the green yarn next, because she is going to use the dye water left over from the black dye. She calls this the afterbath dye water. She first dyes the yarn yellow with the sagebrush, then boils it in the afterbath dye water to give the final green color. Again she selects an enamel vessel for dyeing, because she wants a clear, bright yellow when it is finished; if she had wished to have a mustard yellow she would have used a tin or aluminum kettle. She weighs the sagebrush, adds the water, and boils it for about two hours, after which she strains out the twigs and adds the raw alum, which she has thrown on hot coals until it started to foam. This she stirs well and boils a few minutes, then adds her wet yarn, stirring as she adds it to be sure that it takes the dye evenly. She boils it about three hours and then lifts it out into the black afterbath dye water which she has brought to a boil. She stirs this well and boils it two hours longer, then lets it stay in the dyebath overnight. In the morning she rinses it and hangs it up to dry.

She dyes her brown yarn just as she did her yellow, except that she uses juniper-ash water for her mordant, instead of raw alum. Just before she is ready to add this to the dyebath, she sets fire to a big handful of juniper branches, burning only the green needles, and holds them over a frying pan so that the ashes will fall into it. Then she adds boiling water and, after straining the mixture, uses it as a mordant with mountain mahogany root bark.

The white yarn is the last prepared. She throws the crystal rock of gypsum on the coals until it turns white, and, after it cools, she grinds it to a powder between Navajo grinding stones. She then measures it and stirs it into the water and rinses her natural cream-colored yarn in the solution. When it dries, it will be much whiter, because the gypsum forms a film over the wool.

With her supply of yarn, Mrs. Bryan is now ready to do her weaving.

The finished rug sells by weight and commands a higher price than a rug of equal weight made from undyed or analine-dyed wool. Much more time and effort have gone into the preparation of the yarn, and the total effect of these soft, lustrous colors blended in a simple design makes an art product that is sought by buyers in spite of the greater cost.

Additional Observations Regarding Native Dyes

Dyeing with native dyes is slow and arduous, as shown by the above description. Many laws of chemistry are involved in the process, but the facts were discovered by the Navajo through trial and error. A number of interesting observations, not included in the above discussion, have been made during the experiments and are listed below:

1. The same species of plant grown in different sections of the country may give different shades of color. The shade of color may also vary from year to year from a plant grown in the same locality.

2. All dye plants may be used for dyeing with or without a mordant. The use of a mordant deepens the color and occasionally changes it. The use of a different mordant, or varying the quantity of mordant used, also produces a difference in the color given by the same plant. Colors dyed without a mordant are reasonably fast.

3. Longer boiling of the dye with the yarn usually produces a deeper color. Occasionally the color is entirely changed.

4. Allowing the yarn to remain in the dyebath overnight deepens and brightens the color. It is believed that it also produces a faster color.

5. It is necessary that most of the dyes be boiled with the yarn to produce the color. There are exceptions to this, however. Cactus fruit, some berries, and flowers lose their color when boiled. For this reason we allow the dye to ferment into the yarn, as explained in the recipes.

6. The afterbath yarn, or the second yarn dyed in the same dye water, is a softer, lighter tint of the same color.

7. Most of the plants may be used either fresh or dried. Fresh plants are usually stronger than dried ones. Therefore, less of the fresh plant is required to produce the same color. Dried canyaigre root, however, is stronger than the fresh root. One must bear this in mind when substituting in the following recipes.

8. Dried barks, plants, and fruits should be soaked overnight before using.

9.   Yarns must be rinsed several times after dyeing to remove the unabsorbed dye.

10.   The yarns dyed by the following recipes have been tested for color fastness when treated with commercial cleaners and moth preventives and were found to be unchanged by them.

Preparing Wool

Wool must be cleaned before carding. It may be either dry-cleaned or washed with either of the two occurrent soapplant species, narrow-leaf soapplant, Spanish *amole,* tsa'aszi'ds'ooz (*Yucca glauca*), or wide-leaf soapplant, Spanish popularly *látil,* dictionary-Spanish *dátil,* tsa'aszi'ntxyeelih (*Yucca baccata*). Wool that is dry-cleaned before carding makes a smoother yarn than that which is washed, and so all of it not too dirty is treated this way. The coarse dirt and much of the grease is removed during this process.
TO DRY-CLEAN WOOL

Spread the fleece in the sun, either on brush, rocks, or sand, shorn (cut) side up. Shake while spreading it. In addition, sprinkle it with white clay or toasted pulverized gypsum. (These two materials and their methods of preparation are described under "Whitening Wool.") After a thorough sunning shake the fleece until the dirt falls out.
TO WASH YARN

It is necessary that yarn be clean before it is dyed. For this reason it is washed *after* spinning and *before* dyeing. The only soap that the ancient Navajo knew was obtained from the two soapweeds mentioned above. The roots of these yuccas contain the compound saponin and make an excellent soap, which is still preferred to the commercial article for washing wool.

Látil and *amole* are sword-leaved plants and grow about two feet high. The former has a wide blade and the latter a narrow one. *Látil* grows commonly throughout the reservation between 4,500 and 8,000 feet altitude and *amole* from 3,000 to 7,500 feet.

Both may be used either fresh or dried and may be dug at any time of year when there is not too much frost in the ground. *Amole* root is simply dug and crushed and dried in the sun if it is to be kept for any length of time. *Látil* is treated in the same way, except that it is heated well over hot coals or a stove after being crushed and before it is dried or used fresh. Heating in this way produces a better lather.

Látil is stronger and is preferred by many for washing wool.

If one washes white and light-colored yarns with either of the two soapplants, the yarns do not absorb the grease from the weaver's hands, but when soap is used for the entire washing without a finishing rinse in soap-plant suds, the yarns absorb oil from the weaver's hands and become soiled in appearance.

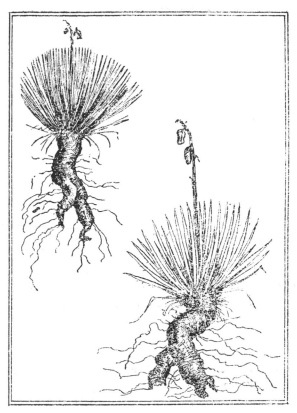

TO WASH YARN WITH YUCCA ROOT

1   handful crushed yucca root (fresh or dried)
1   quart cold water
Sufficient hot water to wash the yarn
1   pound yarn

Free hands and tub from grease, as yucca roots will not lather when grease is present.

Rub the crushed roots between the hands in the cold water until there is a heavy lather. Strain. Add enough hot water to make a warm solution. Wash the yarn thoroughly, using a second suds water if necessary to clean it. Rinse twice.

The finest yarn is washed after spinning, but if the wool is very dirty it must be washed before carding. In that case great care must be taken not to twist or press it hard, as this felts the wool and makes it form lumps. It must be floated around loosely in the water and removed carefully (not wrung) and placed on screens, boards, rocks, or sand to drain and dry.

Selecting and Mixing Natural Colors of Wool

Lovely black (brown-black), tan, brown, and cream colors can be obtained naturally from sheep of various colors.

GRAY

¼ pound black wool

¾ pound cream wool

Mix black and cream wool together and card. Pull to pieces, mix again, and card again to get even color. The proportion of black used will determine the resulting shade of gray.

BROWN

½ pound natural brown wool

½ pound natural tan wool

Prepare same as for gray wool. This makes a very pleasing shade of brown.

TAN

½ pound natural brown wool

½ pound natural cream-color wool

Prepare as for gray wool.

Whitening Wool

½ cup white clay (dleesh), or 2 tablespoons ground, toasted gypsum (selenite variety) (tsesǫ́')

2 cups water

1 pound yarn (natural cream color)

Dissolve the clay or the gypsum in the water and rinse the yarn in it. This will make a white rather than a cream yarn.

So-called white clay is mostly a marl (calcium carbonate). It is found in arid regions throughout the Navajo country as a vein around the tablelands. The Navajo have definite places where they dig it.

Gypsum of the selenite variety is found in small quantities here and there in some shales associated with coal deposits in New Mexico. The Navajo pick it up around coal mines. It has a crystalline appearance. It is toasted by throwing it into the fire or baking it in the oven until it turns white. It is ground into a fine powder between Navajo grinding stones before it is used.

Mordants

ASHES OF JUNIPER
(*JUNIPERUS MONOSPERMA*)
gad bididze' doo bilatxahi bileeshch'iih bitxoo'

The Navajo commonly, but mistakenly, call this juniper cedar. It is also called desert or one-seeded juniper. It is an evergreen tree which grows five feet and higher, depending upon the amount of moisture. It grows plentifully in the foothills of the mountains and on high mesas from 5,000 to 8,000 feet elevation. The ashes from the green needles are used to make the juniper-ash water. The branches may be gathered at any time of year.

To Use Water from Juniper Ashes

1   cup hot juniper ashes

2   cups boiling water

Gather juniper branches from trees that have a reddish appearance. Set fire to a handful and hold them over a skillet to catch the ashes. Burn only the green needles. To the hot ashes add the boiling water. Stir thoroughly and strain. This water is used as a mordant.

Raw Alum
tsekhǫ'

Raw alum is a low-grade, naturally occurring alum. It is found in the form of soft white chunks and is gathered from under large rocks in the flat reservation country where there has been recent water evaporation. It is especially plentiful around the sulphur-spring deposits in New Mexico.

To Use Raw Alum:

Throw the chunks of alum onto hot coals until they start to foam. Then drop them into the dyebath or if desired add them to the dyebath without toasting. The latter method is easier when the dyeing is being done on a stove and is quite satisfactory.

The Dyeing of Yarns:

Recipes

ACTINEA, SEVERAL-FLOWERED
(*ACTINEA LEPTOCLADA*)
bee'ooĺtsoih bee 'iiĺkhoh

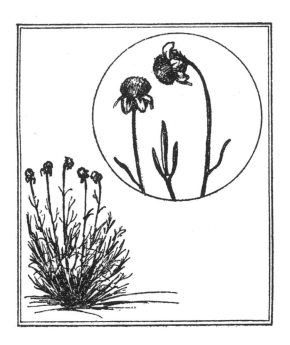

This entire plant is used for dye while in bloom. It grows under the timber in the mountains and reaches a height of about one foot. A number of medium-size, single-petal yellow flowers shoot out from the root.

COLOR 1—*Light Greenish Yellow*

2 pounds *Actinea leptoclada* (blossoms and leaves)

¼ cup raw alum

1 pound yarn

Boil blossoms and leaves in 5 gallons of water in a tin or aluminum vessel for two hours. Strain. Add the raw alum to the dye water. Stir and boil 10 minutes. Add the wet yarn and stir again. Let boil 15 minutes for this tint. Remove immediately from dyebath and rinse.

Note: This dye water may be used a second time for a lighter tint.

ACTINEA, SINGLE-FLOWERED
(*ACTINEA GAILLARDIA*)
be'oochidi bee 'iiłkhoh

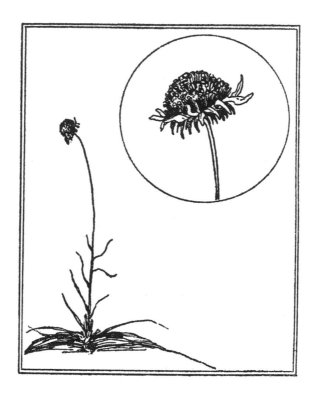

The flowers, leaves, and stems of this plant are used for dye while fresh. It grows about one and a half feet tall under the timber in the mountains. One yellow blossom is sent up from each root. It blooms in June.

COLOR 2—*Yellow*

1   pound *Actinea gaillardia* (flowers, stems, and leaves)

¼   cup raw alum

1   pound yarn

Boil the flowers, leaves, and stems in 5 gallons of water in an enamel or granite vessel for 2 hours. Strain. Add the raw alum to the dye water. Stir and let boil 10 minutes. Add wet yarn. Stir well. Boil 2 hours. Leave in dye-bath overnight. Rinse.

ALDER
(*ALNUS TENUIFOLIA*)
g'ish

The bark of the male tree is the part used for the dye. It is peeled from the limbs while fresh, and dried unless used immediately. The bark gives the strongest color if it is taken in the fall.

The tree grows plentifully along streams in the mountains and reaches a height of twelve feet.

COLOR 3—*Soft Brown*

2   pounds alder bark (from male tree)

1   pound yarn

Soak dried alder bark overnight, then boil for 2 hours in 5 gallons of water. Strain. Add wet yarn and stir well. Boil for 2 hours. Leave in the dye-bath overnight if desired. Rinse.

COLOR 4—*Tan-Beige*

Afterbath dye water (from "Soft Brown" above)

¼ cup raw alum
1 pound yarn

After removing the first pound of yarn, add ¼ cup raw alum to the remaining dye water. Stir well. Let boil 10 minutes. Add wet yarn. Stir again. Boil 2 hours. Leave in the dyebath overnight if desired. Rinse.

Alder bark is also used with mountain mahogany root to produce several shades of tan and brown. The recipes for these dyes are given under "Mahogany, Mountain."

BEE PLANT, ROCKY MOUNTAIN
(*CLEOME SERRULATA*)
waa'

Bee plant is highly esteemed by the Navajo people, because it has saved the tribe at times from starvation. It grows about three feet high and its purple blossoms color sections of the mesas of the reservation through July and August. The entire plant, before it blossomed, was used for the dye given below.

COLOR 7—*Pale Greenish Yellow*

Prepare as for "Greenish Yellow" except that the yarn is boiled only ½ hour and removed immediately from the dyebath.

COLOR 8—*Mustard*

Prepare as for "Greenish Yellow" except that the yarn is dyed in a tin or aluminum vessel.

BITTERBALL
(*TAGETES MICRANTHA*)
bįį yildjaa'ih

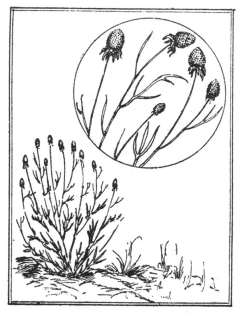

This entire plant while in blossom is used for dye. It grows about two feet high and blooms in early summer. It is a sacred medicine plant, and will probably never be a popular dye plant with the Navajo.

COLOR 6—*Greenish Yellow*

3 pounds bitterball (entire plant)

½ cup raw alum

1 pound yarn

Boil the leaves and twigs in 6 gallons of water for 1 to 2 hours. Strain. Add the alum. Stir well and boil 10 minutes. Add the wet yarn and stir again. Boil 1 to 3 hours, depending upon the depth of color desired. Allowing it to remain in the dyebath overnight will also deepen and brighten the color. Fewer blossoms will make a lighter shade. Boil in an enamel vessel for this bright yellow color. Rinse.

COLOR 5—*Yellow Green*

1 bushel bee plant

1 pound yarn

Boil bee plant in 5 gallons of water until very tender. Mash up the leaves and remove the stalks. Add wet yarn and set in a warm place to ferment for 1 week. Rub the dye into the yarn often. Place yarn in dyebath on the stove and let boil for 1 hour. Remove from the fire and allow to ferment another week in the same dyebath. Rinse.

Cactus, Prickly-Pear
(*Opuntia polycantha*)
hwoshntxyeeli binesd'ą'

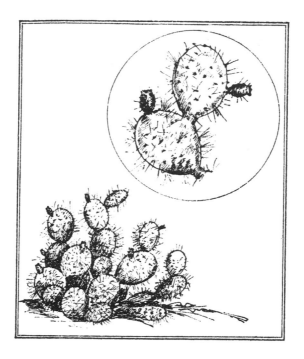

The prickly pear is a low-growing cactus, widely distributed on the mesas of New Mexico and Arizona. It has a yellow blossom and a red fruit which ripens the latter part of September. After picking, the fruit must be rubbed in the sand with the foot to remove the spines. It is then used either fresh or sundried, but it requires more of the dried fruit than of the fresh to give the same color.

COLOR 9—*Rose*

2 pounds fresh cactus fruit (3 if dried)

1 pound yarn

Squeeze the juice from the fruit and strain into 3 gallons of cool water. (If the fruit has been dried, soak before squeezing.) Add wet yarn. Let stand in a warm place for a week to ferment. Rub the dye into the yarn often. Rinse.

Note: This dye cannot be boiled. To do so causes it to lose its color and the yarn becomes tan instead. The fermentation must take place in an earthenware or enamel kettle. If done in tin or aluminum, the color is lost.

COLOR 10—*Deep Rose*

Prepare in the same manner as for "Rose" except that the rose yarn is put into a second dyebath of the same strength as the first and allowed to ferment in it for a second week.

COLOR 11—*Light Rose*

Afterbath dye water from the "Rose" recipe given above

1   pound yarn

Add the wet yarn to the afterbath dye water and proceed in a manner similar to the directions given in the "Rose" recipe.

COLOR 12—*Pink with a Tan Tint*

2   pounds fresh cactus fruit
1   pound yarn

Boil 1 pound of the cactus fruit in 4 gallons of water for 1 hour and strain. Add wet yarn. Boil 1 to 2 hours. This makes a tan yarn. Now squeeze the juice from the other pound of cactus fruit and strain into 3 gallons lukewarm water. Add the tan yarn. Let stand in a warm place for a week to ferment. Rub the yarn often to work the dye into it. Rinse well.

COLOR 13—*Tan*

1   pound cactus fruit
1   pound yarn

Boil the cactus fruit in 4 gallons of water for 1 hour and strain. Bring dye water to a boil. Add wet yarn. Stir well. Boil 1 to 2 hours. Leave in dyebath overnight. Rinse thoroughly.

CACTUS FRUIT AND MOUNTAIN MAHOGANY ROOT BARK
AFTERBATH DYE WATERS

COLOR 14—*Coral Pink*

1½   gallons afterbath dye water (from "Rose" color above)
1½   gallons afterbath dye water (from "Mountain Mahogany Root Bark" recipe found under "Mahogany")
¼   pound yarn

Mix afterbath dye waters together while cold. Do not heat. Add wet yarn. Stir well. Allow to ferment in a warm place for four days or longer if a deeper shade is desired. Rub the yarn often to work the dye into it. Rinse well.

Prickly-pear-cactus fruit is also used with mountain mahogany root bark to obtain a rose taupe and a soft reddish tan. The recipes for these dyes are given under "Mahogany."

CANYAIGRE
(*RUMEX HYMENOSEPALUS*)
chaąd'iniih

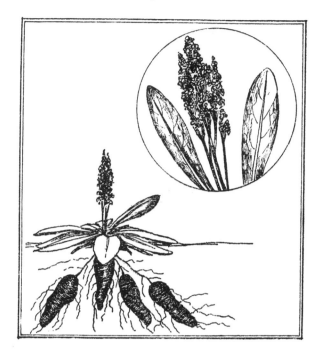

Canyaigre grows on sandy mesas on the reservation. It is a large native dock with leaves which grow about two inches in width, dark green in color and meaty in substance. It has one flower stock arising from the center. The roots of the plant, which are the part used for dye, resemble sweet potatoes, and are very rich in tannic acid. They may be used fresh or after having been split and sundried.

COLOR 15—*Medium Brown*

1   pound dried canyaigre roots
1   pound yarn

Boil canyaigre roots in 4 gallons of water for 1 hour. Mash to liberate the dye substances. Strain. Add wet yarn. Stir well. Boil 1 to 2 hours. Leave in dyebath overnight if a deeper color is desired. Rinse.

COLOR 16—*Yellow-Orange*

½   pound canyaigre roots
¼   cup raw alum
1   pound yarn

Boil the canyaigre roots in 4 gallons of water for 1 hour. Mash to liberate dye substances. Strain. Add alum. Let boil. Stir well. Add wet yarn. Stir again. Boil 1 to 2 hours. Leave in dyebath overnight if a deeper color is desired.

CELERY, WILD
(*PSEUDOCYMOPTERUS MONTANUS*)
haza'aleehtsoh

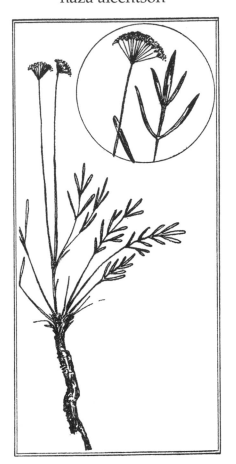

This is a frail-looking plant which is found in the timber regions in the mountains. It grows about one foot high and blooms in June and July. The entire plant is used for dye while fresh.

COLOR 17—*Light Canary Yellow*

1   pound wild celery (flowers and leaves)
¼   cup raw alum
1   pound yarn

Boil wild celery flowers and leaves in 5 gallons of water in a tin or aluminum vessel for two hours. Strain. Add the raw alum to the dye water. Stir and let boil 10 minutes. Add wet yarn and stir well. Let boil 15 minutes. Remove immediately from dyebath and rinse.

Note: This dye water may be used to color a second pound of yarn a lighter tint.

CHAMIZO
(*ATRIPLEX CANESCENS*)
diwozhiiłbaih

This shrub is always green and its leaves and twigs may be gathered any time for dye. The blossoms are also used when present on the plant. It grows about three feet high and is common on the mesas throughout New Mexico and Arizona. There are male and female plants of this species and either is suitable.

COLOR 18—*Bright Yellow*

3   pounds chamizo leaves, twigs, and blossoms
½   cup raw alum
1   pound yarn

Boil the blossoms and twigs in 6 gallons of water for 1 to 2 hours. Strain. Add the alum. Stir well and boil 10 minutes. Add the wet yarn and stir again. Boil 1 to 3 hours, depending upon the depth of color desired. Allowing it to remain in the dyebath overnight will also deepen and brighten the color. Fewer blossoms will make a lighter shade. Boil in an enamel vessel for this bright yellow color. Rinse.

COLOR 19—*Light Canary Yellow*

Prepare as for "Bright Yellow" except that the yarn is boiled only ½ hour and removed immediately from the dyebath.

COLOR 20—*Mustard*

Prepare as for "Bright Yellow" except that the yarn is dyed in a tin or aluminum vessel.

CHOKECHERRY
(*PRUNUS MELANOCARPA*)
didzedig'ozhiih

The chokecherry is found in middle elevations in the mountains. It grows about eight to ten feet tall. The bark and roots are suitable for dye purposes.

CHOKECHERRY ROOT BARK AND WILD PLUM ROOT BARK

COLOR 21—*Purplish Brown*

1 pound chokecherry root bark
1 pound wild plum root bark
1 pound yarn

Break up the bark after peeling it from the roots. Add 5 gallons water and let soak overnight. Boil for 2 hours. Strain. Add wet yarn to the dye water and stir well. Boil 2 hours. Let remain in dyebath overnight. Rinse.

CLAW, OWL'S
(*HELENIUM HOOPESII*)
g'asdah bee gạh

This plant is a favorite yellow-dye plant with the Navajo. It grows about three feet high. It has long narrow leaves and one yellow blossom on each flower stem. It is found in the meadows in the high mountains and blooms the latter part of June or the first part of July. The entire plant when in blossom is used for dye purposes while fresh.

COLOR 22—*Bright Yellow*

3   pounds owl's claw (leaves, twigs, and blossoms)
½   cup raw alum
1   pound yarn

Boil the blossoms and twigs in 6 gallons of water for 1 to 2 hours. Strain. Add the alum. Stir well and boil 10 minutes. Add the wet yarn and stir again. Boil 1 to 3 hours, depending upon the depth of color desired. Allowing it to remain in the dyebath overnight will also deepen and brighten the color. Fewer blossoms will make a lighter shade. Boil in an enamel vessel for this bright yellow color. Rinse.

COLOR 23—*Light Canary Yellow*

Prepare as for "Bright Yellow" except that the yarn is boiled only ½ hour and removed immediately from the dyebath.

COLOR 24—*Mustard*

Prepare as for "Bright Yellow" except that the yarn is dyed in a tin or aluminum vessel.

GRAPE, OREGON
(BERBERIS AQUIFOLIUM)
chech'il ntł'izi yild'aą'ih

The Oregon grape grows commonly in the mountains at 8,000 feet altitude and above. The entire plant was used for the dye described below. It may be used fresh or dried.

COLOR 25—*Dulled Greenish Yellow*

4   pounds Oregon grape (roots, leaves, and stems)
¼   cup raw alum
1   pound yarn

Boil Oregon grape vines in 5 gallons of water in a granite vessel for 2 hours. Strain. Add the raw alum to the dye water. Stir and let boil 10 minutes. Add wet yarn. Stir again. Leave in dyebath overnight. Rinse.

IRONWOOD OR WILD PRIVET
(*FORESTIERA NEOMEXICANA*)
mą'iidąą' or g'iishzniniih

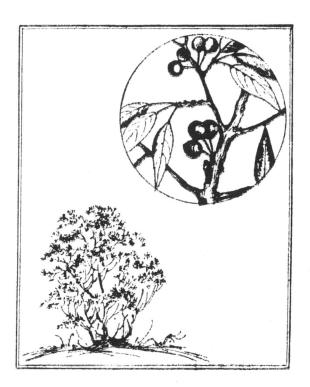

The first Navajo name means coyote food. The ironwood tree grows on the foothills of the mountains. The red fruit ripens the latter part of August and turns blue when it is dead ripe. The Navajo use the berries and twigs for ceremonial purposes and for this reason they will not eat them. The very ripe berries are used in making this gray dye.

COLOR 26—*Light Gray*

2 pounds ripe ironwood berries
1 pound yarn

Boil berries 15 minutes in 4 gallons of water. Strain. Add wet yarn and stir well. Boil ½ hour. Remove from fire and allow to ferment in the dyebath 4 days for this shade. Rinse.

Juniper, One-Seeded
(*Juniperus monosperma*)
gad

This tree has been described under "Mordants."

The bast and twigs and the berries, if desired, may be used for dye.

COLOR 27—*Orange-Tan*

2 pounds juniper bast and twigs

¼ cup raw alum

1 pound yarn

Boil juniper bast and twigs in 4 gallons of water for 1 hour. Strain. Add alum and let boil. Stir well. Add wet yarn and stir again. Boil 1 to 2 hours, depending upon depth of color desired. Leave in dye water overnight. Rinse.

COLOR 28—*Yellow-Tan*

Prepare in the same manner as for "Orange-Tan," but omit the raw alum and use no mordant.

LARKSPUR, WILD PURPLE
(*DELPHINIUM SCAPOSUM*)
txadidii̧dootł'izh

This dainty plant with a purple flower grows in timber on the desert where there is a little moisture. It is a sacred plant to the Navajo, its purple petals being used in some of their ceremonies. For this reason many Navajo will not use it for dye. It has been reported that the purple petals yield a purple dye. The experiments at the school have failed to give a color even approaching it either by fermenting the plant or boiling it. The purple petals or the entire plant may be used for dye.

COLOR 29—*Greenish Gray*

2 pounds purple larkspur petals
1 pound yarn

Pour enough warm water over the petals to cover. Soak 1 day and then mash them. Add wet yarn and allow to ferment in a warm place for 1 week. Work the dye into the yarn often. Rinse.

COLOR 30—*Light Greenish Yellow*

2 pounds purple larkspur (flowers, leaves, stems)
¼ cup raw alum
1 pound yarn

Boil larkspur in 5 gallons of water in a granite or enamel vessel for 2 hours. Strain. Add the raw alum to the dye water. Stir and let boil 10 minutes. Add wet yarn. Stir again. Boil 2 hours. Leave in dyebath overnight. Rinse.

Lichen, Ground
(*Parmelia molluscula*)
nị 'hadlaad

These tiny plants cling to the ground under sagebrush and trees on certain mesas in the Southwest. The entire plant is boiled for dye. They may be used fresh or dried.

Stone lichen (tsedlaad) may be similarly used. They grow on stones in the foothills of the mountains in the Southwest and are easily scraped off after a rain loosens them.

COLOR 31—*Light Orange*

2   pounds ground lichens
¼   cup raw alum
1   pound yarn

Boil lichens in 4 gallons of water for 1 hour. Strain. Add alum and let boil. Stir well. Add wet yarn and stir again. Boil ½ hour. Rinse.

COLOR 32—*Reddish Tan*

½   pound ground lichens
¼   cup raw alum
1   pound yarn

Boil lichens in 4 gallons of water for 1 hour. Strain. Add alum and let boil. Stir well. Add wet yarn and stir again. Boil 1 to 2 hours, depending upon depth of color desired. Less alum and a shorter boiling time produces a lighter color. Leaving it in the dyebath overnight gives a deeper shade. Rinse.

COLOR 33—*Yellow-Tan*

Prepare as for "Reddish Tan" except that the water from 1 cup juniper ashes is used instead of raw alum as a mordant.

Ground lichens may also be used with mountain mahogany root to produce light red-brown. The recipe for this dye is given under "Mahogany."

LUPINE, BLUE-FLOWERED
(*LUPINUS KINGII*)
'azee' diilch'ił iih or łįį'daą'

Lupines grow quite commonly in the mountains and reach a height of one and a half to two feet. They begin to bloom in June and the entire plants are used while fresh.

COLOR 34—*Greenish Yellow*

4 pounds lupine (flowers, leaves, stems)

¼ cup raw alum

1 pound yarn

Boil the flowers, leaves, and stems in 5 gallons of water in an enamel or granite vessel for 2 hours. Strain. Add the raw alum to the dye water. Stir and let boil 10 minutes. Add wet yarn. Stir well. Boil 2 hours. Leave in dyebath overnight. Rinse.

MAHOGANY, MOUNTAIN
(*CERCOCARPUS MONTANUS*)
tse 'esdaaziih

The bark of the root of this tree is red and is the part used for dye. It gives the strongest color when dug in the fall.

The tree, which grows four to eight feet in height, is found commonly in the mountains and on the foothills at an elevation of 7,000 to 10,000 feet.

MOUNTAIN MAHOGANY ROOT BARK

COLOR 35—*Soft Reddish Brown*

2   pounds mountain mahogany root bark

1   pound yarn

Boil mountain mahogany root bark for 2 hours in 5 gallons of water. Strain. Add wet yarn and boil for 2 hours. Stir well. Leave in dyebath overnight. Rinse thoroughly.

MOUNTAIN MAHOGANY ROOT BARK (*WITH JUNIPER ASHES*)

COLOR 36—*Deep Reddish Brown*

2   pounds mountain mahogany root bark

Water from 1 cup juniper ashes

1   pound yarn

Boil mountain mahogany root bark in 5 gallons of water for 2 hours. Strain. Add juniper-ash water to the dyebath. (The method of preparation is described under "Mordants.") Stir and boil 15 minutes. Add wet yarn and stir well. Boil 1 hour and leave in the dyebath overnight. Rinse thoroughly.

MOUNTAIN MAHOGANY ROOT BARK AND CACTUS FRUIT NO. 1

COLOR 37—*Rose Taupe*

1 pound mountain mahogany root bark
1 pound dried prickly-pear-cactus fruit
Water from one cup juniper ashes
1 pound yarn

Boil the mountain mahogany for an hour in 5 gallons of water. Strain. Cool until likewarm. Soak the cactus fruit in 1 quart of water overnight and strain, squeezing the pulp through. Combine with the mountain mahogany solution. Add the wet yarn, which has been soaked for a few minutes in the juniper-ash water. Allow to ferment in a warm place for one week. Rub the dye into the yarn often. Rinse thoroughly.

MOUNTAIN MAHOGANY ROOT BARK AND CACTUS FRUIT NO. 2

COLOR 38—*Soft Reddish Tan*

1 pound mountain mahogany root bark
1 pound dried prickly-pear-cactus fruit
1 pound yarn

Boil the mountain mahogany root bark for an hour in 5 gallons of water. Strain and cool until lukewarm. Soak the cactus fruit in 1 quart of water and strain, squeezing the pulp through. Combine with the mountain mahogany solution. Add wet yarn and allow to ferment in a warm place for 1 week. Rub the dye into the yarn often. Rinse thoroughly.

This makes a beautiful background color.

The afterbath dye water from mountain mahogany root bark and prickly-pear-cactus fruit may be used to obtain a coral pink. The recipe for this dye is given under "Cactus Fruit."

Fresh cactus fruit may be used. The same amount will give a slightly deeper color, or slightly less may be used.

MOUNTAIN MAHOGANY ROOT BARK AND NAVAJO TEA NO. 1

COLOR 39—*Dark Burnt Orange*

1 pound mountain mahogany root bark
2 pounds Navajo tea
½ cup raw alum
1 pound yarn

Soak mountain mahogany root bark and Navajo tea overnight in 5 gallons of water. Boil 1 hour and strain. Bring dye water to a boil and add alum. Stir well and let boil 10 minutes. Add wet yarn and stir again. Boil 2 hours and remove immediately from the dyebath. Rinse well.

MOUNTAIN MAHOGANY ROOT BARK AND NAVAJO TEA NO. 2
COLOR 40—*Henna*

Prepare as for "Mountain Mahogany Root Bark and Navajo Tea No. 1" except that instead of removing the yarn from the dyebath immediately after boiling, allow it to ferment in the dye water for 1 week. Rub the dye into the yarn often. Rinse.

MOUNTAIN MAHOGANY ROOT BARK AND GROUND LICHENS
COLOR 41—*Light Red-Brown*

1 pound mountain mahogany root bark
½ pound ground lichens
Water from 1 cup juniper ashes
1 pound yarn

Boil the bark and the lichens together in 5 gallons of water for 2 hours. Strain. Add juniper-ash water. (The method of preparing juniper-ash water is described under "Mordants.") Stir well. Boil 15 minutes. Add wet yarn and stir again. Boil 2 hours. Leave in the dyebath overnight. Rinse.

MOUNTAIN MAHOGANY ROOT BARK AND ALDER BARK NO. 1
COLOR 42—*Light Brown*

1 pound mountain mahogany root bark
1 pound alder bark
¼ cup raw alum
1 pound yarn

Soak mountain mahogany root bark and alder bark in 5 gallons of water overnight. Boil 1 hour and strain. Then add raw alum and boil 10 minutes, stirring constantly. Add wet yarn. Stir well. Boil 2 hours. Leave in dyebath overnight. Rinse thoroughly.

MOUNTAIN MAHOGANY ROOT BARK AND ALDER BARK NO. 2
COLOR 43—*Reddish Tan*

2 pounds mountain mahogany root bark
½ pound alder bark
1 pound yarn

Soak the two barks in 5 gallons of water overnight. Then boil 1 hour and strain. Bring to a boil and add wet yarn. Stir well. Boil 1 hour and remove from dyebath immediately. Rinse thoroughly.

MOUNTAIN MAHOGANY ROOT BARK AND ALDER BARK NO. 3
COLOR 44—*Soft Cream-Tan*

2 pounds mountain mahogany root bark
½ pound alder bark
1 pound yarn

Soak the barks in 3 gallons of warm water for 1 to 2 days (the color of many plant materials, especially if dried, seems to come out into the water better, if they are allowed to ferment a little before being strained out). Strain. Add wet yarn. Let stand in a warm place for 1 week to ferment. Rub the dye into the yarn often. Rinse well.

MOUNTAIN MAHOGANY ROOT BARK AND ALDER BARK NO. 4
COLOR 45—*Light Brown*

1   pound mountain mahogany root bark
1   cup juniper ashes
½   pound alder bark
1   pound yarn

Boil mountain mahogany and alder barks in 6 gallons of water for 1 hour. Strain. Add water from juniper ashes. (Method of preparation is described under "Mordants.") Boil 15 minutes. Wet the yarn and add it to the dyebath. Stir well. Let boil 2 hours. Rinse thoroughly.

OAK, GAMBEL'S
(*QUERCUS GAMBELII*)
chech'l bikhashd'oozh

The bark of this tree is the part used for dye and gives the strongest color when gathered in the fall. It is stripped from the wood immediately and may be used either fresh or dried. Gambel's oak grows commonly in the lower mountains.

GAMBEL'S OAK BARK

COLOR 46—*Dulled Tan*

8 pounds Gambel's oak bark

½ cup raw alum

1 pound yarn

Pound up the bark and boil in 5 gallons of water for 2 hours. Strain. Add the raw alum to the dye water and boil 10 minutes. Add the wet yarn and stir again. Boil for 2 hours. Allow to remain in the dyebath overnight. Rinse.

OAK, SCRUB
(*QUERCUS PUNGENS*)
chech'ilntł'izih

This scrub tree is found in the low mountains. The gall, which grows on it, is the part used for dye.

GALL FROM SCRUB OAK

COLOR 47—*Light Gold*

4 pounds gall (green or brown)

¼ cup raw alum

1 pound yarn

Pulverize the gall and boil in 5 gallons of water for 2 hours. Strain. Add the raw alum to the dye water and boil 10 minutes. Place the wet yarn into the dyebath and stir well. Boil for 2 hours. Allow to remain in the dye water overnight. Rinse.

COLOR 48—*Light Yellowish Tan*

1 pound gall (green or brown)

¼ cup raw alum

1 pound yarn

Pulverize the gall and boil in 5 gallons of water for 2 hours. Strain. Add raw alum to the dye water. Stir and boil 10 minutes. Place the wet yarn in the dyebath and stir well. Boil for 2 hours. Allow to remain in the dyebath overnight. Rinse.

PAINTBRUSH, INDIAN
(*CASTILLEJA INTEGRE*)
dahitxįhidaą'

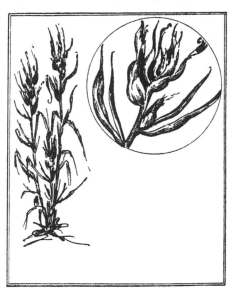

The Navajo name means hummingbird food. It grows from one to one and a half feet tall and is found in the lower parts of the mountains. Either the flowers alone or the entire plant may be used for dye purposes. It blooms in June and July and is used while fresh.

INDIAN PAINTBRUSH BLOSSOMS

COLOR 49—*Tan*

4   pounds Indian paintbrush blossoms
Cold water to cover
1   pound yarn

Pour enough cold water over the blossoms to cover. Soak a day or two and mash up the blossoms. Remove hard stems. Add wet yarn to dyebath and allow to ferment in a warm place for 1 week. Work the dye into the yarn often. Rinse.

INDIAN PAINTBRUSH (ENTIRE PLANT)

COLOR 50—*Greenish Yellow*

2   pounds Indian paintbrush (stems, leaves, and blossoms)
¼   cup raw alum
1   pound yarn

Boil Indian paintbrush in 5 gallons of water in an enamel or granite vessel for 2 hours. Strain. Add the raw alum to the dye water. Stir and let boil 10 minutes. Add wet yarn and stir again. Boil 2 hours. Leave in dyebath overnight. Rinse.

PINEDROPS
(*PTEROSPORA ANDROMEDEA*)
ndoochii'

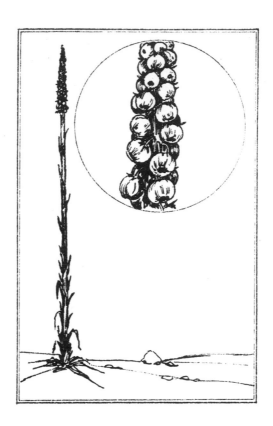

This plant, which is found in the open woods, presents an unusual appearance. It grows about two feet high, and has a reddish-brown stalk with round, drop-like brown berries shooting out on all sides on the upper part of the stalk. It is gathered in the late summer or early fall and may be used either fresh or dried. The entire plant is made into the dye.

COLOR 51—*Dull Tan*

1   pound dry pinedrops (entire plant)

¼   cup raw alum

1   pound yarn

Pulverize the plant and boil in 5 gallons of water for 2 hours. Strain. Add the raw alum to the dye water. Stir and boil 10 minutes. Place the wet yarn in the dyebath and stir again. Boil for 2 hours. Allow to remain in the dyebath overnight. Rinse.

PLUM, WILD
(*PRUNUS AMERICANA*)
didzeh

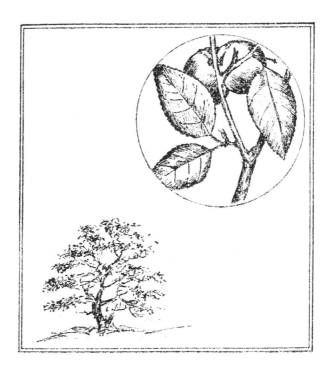

The wild plum is not common on the reservation but has been introduced in some places. The tree grows five to eight feet high. The roots give the purple dye.

WILD PLUM ROOTS

COLOR 52—*Reddish Purple*

2   pounds wild-plum roots

¼   cup raw alum

1   pound yarn

Boil the roots in 6 gallons of water for 1 to 2 hours. Strain. Add the alum. Stir well and boil 10 minutes. Add the wet yarn and stir again. Boil 1 to 3 hours, depending upon the depth of color desired. Leave in dyebath overnight. Rinse.

Rabbitbrush, Big
(*Chrysothamnus latisquameus*)
g'iiɬtsoih

The shrub is found very commonly in arroyos or places where a little water is available. It grows four or five feet in height and is covered with fluffy yellow blossoms in the late summer and early fall. The flowers and twigs, while fresh, are used for dye.

COLOR 53—*Bright Yellow*

3 pounds rabbitbrush blossoms and twigs

½ cup raw alum

1 pound yarn

Boil the blossoms and twigs in 6 gallons of water for 1 to 2 hours. Strain. Add the alum. Stir well and boil 10 minutes. Add the wet yarn and stir again. Boil 1 to 3 hours, depending upon the depth of color desired. Allowing it to remain in the dyebath overnight will also deepen and brighten the color. Fewer blossoms will make a lighter shade. Boil in an enamel vessel for this bright yellow color. Rinse.

COLOR 54—*Light Canary Yellow*

Prepare as for "Bright Yellow" except that the yarn is boiled only ½ hour and removed immediately from the dyebath.

COLOR 55—*Mustard*

Prepare as for "Bright Yellow" except that the yarn is dyed in a tin or aluminum vessel.

RABBITBRUSH, SMALL
(*CHRYSOTHAMNUS BIGELOVII*)
g'iiłtsoididjoolih

This species of rabbitbrush is found out on the flat open mesas but is not very common. It grows about two feet high and blooms during the late summer and early fall. The twigs and blossoms are used for dye.

COLOR 56—*Bright Yellow*

3   pounds rabbitbrush blossoms and twigs
½   cup raw alum
1   pound yarn

Boil the blossoms and twigs in 6 gallons of water for 1 to 2 hours. Strain. Add the alum. Stir well and boil 10 minutes. Add the wet yarn and stir again. Boil 1 to 3 hours, depending upon the depth of color desired. Allowing it to remain in the dyebath overnight will also deepen and brighten the color. Fewer blossoms will make a lighter shade. Boil in an enamel vessel for this bright yellow color. Rinse.

COLOR 57—*Light Canary Yellow*

Prepare as for "Bright Yellow" except that the yarn is boiled only ½ hour and removed immediately from the dyebath.

COLOR 58—*Mustard*

Prepare as for "Bright Yellow" except that the yarn is dyed in a tin or aluminum vessel.

ROSE, CLIFF
(*COWANIA STANSBURIANA*)
'awee'ds'aal

Cliff rose is a signal plant to the Navajo. If it blooms late in October, it is believed to indicate that there will be deep snow during the winter. Its little white blossoms appear in the early summer. Its evergreen twigs may be used for dye at any season of the year. It grows commonly on the lower parts of the mountains.

COLOR 59—*Gold*

2 pounds fresh cliff rose (twigs and leaves)

¼ cup raw alum

1 pound yarn

Boil the twigs and leaves in 5 gallons of water for 2 hours. Strain. Add raw alum to the dye water. Stir and let boil 10 minutes. Add the wet yarn and stir again. Boil for 2 hours. Allow to remain in the dyebath overnight. Rinse.

RUBBERPLANT
(*HYMENOXYS METCALFEI*)
ne'eshdjaa' yilkhyee'eh

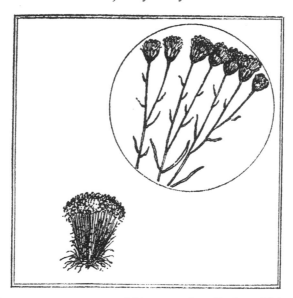

The Navajo name means resembling eared owl's foot. This plant, which blooms in July and August, grows to be about one foot high. It is very common in the timber regions on the mountains. It is a rubberplant, although not the Colorado rubberplant which is so common throughout New Mexico. The leaves, stems, and yellow flowers are used for dye and may be either fresh or dried.

COLOR 60—*Bright Yellow*

3   pounds rubberplant (leaves, stems, and flowers)

½   cup raw alum

1   pound yarn

Boil the blossoms and twigs in 6 gallons of water for 1 to 2 hours. Strain. Add the alum. Stir well and boil 10 minutes. Add the wet yarn and stir again. Boil 1 to 3 hours, depending upon the depth of color desired. Allowing it to remain in the dyebath overnight will also deepen and brighten the color. Fewer blossoms will make a lighter shade. Boil in an enamel vessel for this bright yellow color. Rinse.

COLOR 61—*Light Canary Yellow*

Prepare as for "Bright Yellow" except that the yarn is boiled only ½ hour and removed immediately from the dyebath.

COLOR 62—*Mustard*

Prepare as for "Bright Yellow" except that the yarn is dyed in a tin or aluminum vessel.

Sagebrush, Basin
(*Artemisia tridentata*)
ds'ah

This shrub grows three to four feet high. It is one of the most characteristic plants between 4,500 and 8,000 feet altitude in northern and northwestern New Mexico. The Navajo consider it a very valuable plant, because it is used for medicine and forage as well as for dye. It is always green and its leaves and twigs may be used the year round.

COLOR 63—*Slightly Greenish Yellow*

3   pounds sagebrush leaves and twigs
½   cup raw alum
1   pound yarn

Boil the leaves and twigs in 6 gallons of water for 1 to 2 hours. Strain. Add the alum. Stir well and boil 10 minutes. Add the wet yarn and stir again. Boil 1 to 3 hours, depending upon the depth of color desired. Allowing it to remain in the dyebath overnight will also deepen and brighten the color. Fewer twigs will make a lighter shade. Boil in an enamel vessel for this bright yellow color. Rinse.

COLOR 64—*Pale Greenish Yellow*

Prepare as for "Slightly Greenish Yellow" except that the yarn is boiled only ½ hour and removed immediately from the dyebath.

COLOR 65—*Mustard*

Prepare as for "Slightly Greenish Yellow" except that the yarn is dyed in a tin or aluminum vessel.

COLOR 66—*Gold*

3   pounds sagebrush
½   cup raw alum
1   pound yarn

Boil the twigs and leaves in 5 gallons of water for 2 hours. Strain. Add raw alum to the dye water. Stir and let boil 10 minutes. Add the wet yarn and stir again. Boil gently about 6 hours. Allow to remain in dye water overnight. Rinse.

COLOR 67—*Rich Olive Green*

2   pounds sagebrush
1   cup raw alum
Afterbath black dye water (from recipe given under "Sumac, Piñon, and
    Yellow Ocher").
⅓   pound yarn

Dye the yarn yellow first with sage and alum described above for "Slightly Greenish Yellow." Remove from dyebath and add to the boiling afterbath black dye water. Let boil two hours. Leave in dyebath overnight. Rinse.

COLOR 68—*Medium Olive Green*

4   pounds sagebrush
1   cup raw alum
Afterbath black dye water (from recipe given under "Sumac, Piñon, and
    Yellow Ocher").
1   pound yarn

The method of preparation is the same as for "Rich Olive Green" above.

Sumac, Three-Leaved (*Rhus trilobata*)
chiiłchin or g'ił',
Pitch of the Piñon (*Pinus edulis*)
cha'oł bidjeeh,
and Yellow Ocher
łeetsoh

Sumac

Piñon

Sumac withes with leaves, piñon pitch, and yellow ocher, a mineral, are used in making black dye.

Sumac is also called squaw bush and skunk bush. It is a shrub which grows three to six feet high, depending upon the amount of moisture. It grows wherever a little water is available, as along arroyos and streams. The withes with leaves are used for making black dye and may be either fresh or dried. Before drying, the Navajo twist the twigs into rolls which weigh about ¼ pound each.

The piñon is found on the foothills of the mountains of New Mexico and Arizona at an elevation of 4,000 to 8,000 feet. It is an evergreen tree which grows ten feet and higher, depending upon the amount of moisture. The pitch which oozes out of the tree and collects on the bark is used for this dye.

The mineral, yellow ocher, is a type of gypsum with a little iron in it. It may be picked up around coal mines in the arid regions on the Navajo reservation. It is found in soft yellow chunks.

COLOR 69—*Bluish Black* (generally known as the native black dye)

2   pounds sumac withes with leaves
3   cups piñon pitch
3   cups yellow ocher
1   pound yarn

Roll the sumac in rolls (4 large rolls). In winter use dried leaves only. Boil the sumac with 6 gallons of water from 1 to 3 hours (longer boiling produces a faster color).

Toast the ocher to cocoa brown in a frying pan. Drop in the pitch, a little at a time; stir well as long as it smokes. It should now be shiny like gunpowder and a bluish color. Cool the ocher until just warm before using.

Caution: This is inflammable, so keep it away from flames.

Strain the sumac, add the ocher and pitch, stir and boil 15 minutes. Add wet yarn. Boil 2 to 3 hours. Leave yarn in dye water overnight. Rinse two or three times and dry. Shake or rub in a cloth to remove loose powder.

Note: If any ocher-and-pitch mixture is left over, warm it a little before using it again.

COLOR 70—*Light Oxford Gray*

Afterbath native black dye water from above recipe
1   pound yarn

Add sufficient water to the afterbath black dye water to make 4 gallons. Bring to a boil. Add wet yarn. Stir well. Boil 2 to 3 hours, stirring frequently. For a darker color, allow the yarn to remain in the dyebath overnight. Rinse thoroughly.

SUMAC BERRIES

COLOR 71—*Light Orange-Brown*

4   pounds ripe sumac berries (dried)
1   pound yarn

Grind sumac berries between Navajo grinding stones. Soak in 3 gallons of lukewarm water for 2 days or until sufficient fermentation has taken place so that the color of the fruit has passed out into the dye water. Strain, squeezing the pulp through. Add wet yarn. Let stand in a warm place to ferment. Rub the yarn often to work the dye into it. Rinse well.

TEA, MORMON
(*EPHEDRA VIRIDIS*)
dł'oh'azihih

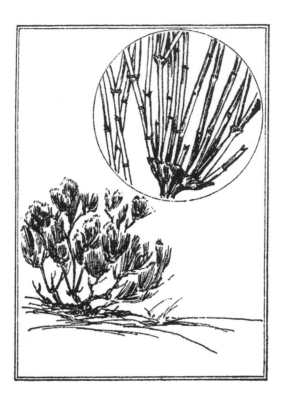

This evergreen shrub grows commonly on the mesas. The twigs with their leaves are used for dye and may be gathered at any time.

COLOR 72—*Light Tan*

2 pounds Mormon tea (twigs and leaves)

¼ cup raw alum

1 pound yarn

Pound the stalks to break them up. Cover with 5 gallons of water and boil 2 hours. Strain. Add raw alum to the dye water. Stir and boil 10 minutes. Place the wet yarn in the dyebath and stir again. Boil 2 hours. Allow to remain in the dyebath overnight. Rinse.

Tea, Navajo
(*THELESPERMA GRACILE*)
ch'ilgohwehih

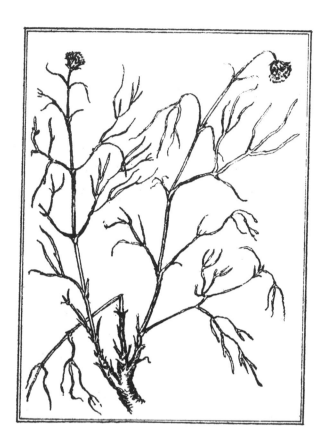

Navajo tea is common in the timber regions on the mountains and around the edges of cultivated land at high elevations if the moisture is sufficient. It grows from one to two feet tall and its orange blossoms appear in July. The leaves, stems, and flowers are used for dye purposes and may be either fresh or dried. The Navajo twist the stems into small uniform-size rolls before drying.

COLOR 73—*Orange*

2   pounds dried Navajo tea

½   cup raw alum

1   pound yarn

Boil tea in 5 gallons of water for 1 hour. Strain. Add alum. Let boil. Stir well. Add wet yarn. Stir again. Boil 2 hours and remove immediately from dyebath for this tone of color. Rinse well.

COLOR 74—*Light Orange*
Afterbath dye water from the Navajo tea in the above recipe
¼ cup raw alum
1 pound yarn

Bring afterbath dye water to a boil and add raw alum. Stir well. Add wet yarn. Stir again. Boil 2 hours and leave in the dyebath overnight. Rinse thoroughly.

COLOR 75—*Light Olive Green*
2 pounds fresh Navajo tea (must be fresh for this color)
1 pound yarn

Boil tea in 4 gallons of water for 1 hour and strain. Add wet yarn. Stir well. Boil 1 hour. Remove immediately from dyebath. Rinse well.

NAVAJO TEA AND CANYAIGRE ROOT

COLOR 76—*Orange*
½ pound fresh Navajo tea
½ pound dried canyaigre root
½ cup raw alum
1 pound yarn

Soak canyaigre root overnight in 5 gallons of water. Then add Navajo tea and boil 1 hour. Strain. Add alum and boil 10 minutes. Stir well. Add wet yarn. Stir again. Boil 1 hour and remove immediately from dyebath. Rinse well.

Navajo tea is also used with mountain mahogany root bark to obtain a dark burnt orange and a henna. The recipes for these dyes are given under "Mahogany."

NAVAJO TEA AND AFTERBATH BLACK DYE WATER

COLOR 77—*Pine-needle Green*
2 pounds Navajo tea
½ cup raw alum
Afterbath black dye water (from recipe given under "Sumac.")
1 pound yarn

Dye the yarn orange first with the Navajo tea and alum as described above for "Orange." Remove from the dyebath and add to the boiling afterbath black dye water. Stir well. Let boil 2 hours. Leave in dyebath overnight. Rinse thoroughly.

THISTLE, RUSSIAN
(*SALSOLA PESTIFER*)
ch'ildeeninih

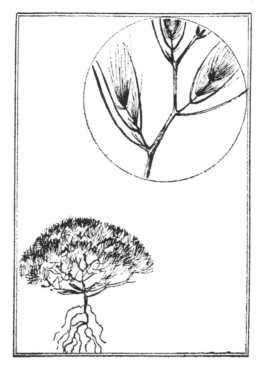

This very troublesome prickly weed grows anywhere at lower altitudes. The entire plant, while young, is used in the recipe given below.

COLOR 78—*Dull Olive Green*

1   bushel Russian thistle (entire plant)

1   pound yarn

Boil the thistle in 5 gallons of water until very tender. Pull out the stalks. Add wet yarn. Allow leaves to ferment in the dyebath with the yarn for 1 week. Rub the dye into the yarn often. Place yarn in dyebath on the stove and let boil 1 hour. Remove from fire and allow to ferment another week in the same dye water. Rinse twice or until water comes out clear.

COLOR 79—*Deep Tan*

½   bushel Russian thistle (young plants)

1   pound yarn

Boil thistle in 5 gallons of water until very tender. Pull out the stalks. Add wet yarn. Allow leaves to ferment in dyebath with yarn for one week. Rub the dye into the yarn often. Place yarn in dyebath on the stove and let boil 1 hour. Remove from fire and allow to ferment another week in the same dye water. Rinse.

Walnut, Wild
(*Juglans Major*)
ha'ałtsedih

The wild-walnut tree is found growing in canyons in New Mexico and Arizona. It grows five to six feet tall and higher where there is more moisture. The leaves, hulls, and the whole nut are used for dye purposes and may either be fresh or dried.

WILD-WALNUT HULLS

COLOR 80—*Rich Brown*

2 pounds wild-walnut hulls

½ cup raw alum

1 pound yarn

Crush the hulls, add 4 gallons of water and let soak overnight. Boil 1 hour longer and strain. Add alum and boil 10 minutes. Stir well. Wet the yarn and place it in the dyebath. Stir and let boil 2 hours. Leave in dyebath overnight. Rinse.

Almost any shade of brown can be made by varying the weight of the hulls used. The entire nut may be used if desired.

Note: If the alum is omitted in the above recipe, the color of the yarn is not as deep nor as rich as when alum is used but tends to be a little more gray in color. This shade of brown blends very nicely with bright colors when used as a background.

COLOR 81—*Gray-Tan*

Afterbath dye water (from "Wild-Walnut Hulls" above)

½ cup raw alum
1 pound yarn

After removing the first pound of yarn, add the raw alum to the remaining dye water. Stir well. Let boil 10 minutes. Add wet yarn. Stir again. Boil 2 hours. Leave in the dyebath overnight. Rinse.

WILD WALNUTS AND HULLS

COLOR 82—*Rich Tan*

1 pound whole walnuts and hulls
¼ cup raw alum
1 pound yarn

Add 4 gallons of water to the hulls and whole walnuts. Soak overnight. Then boil 1 hour. Strain. Add alum and boil 10 minutes. Stir well. Wet the yarn and place it in the dyebath. Stir and let boil 1 hour. Remove immediately from the dyebath. Rinse thoroughly.

Note: Break the nuts in pieces if a darker shade is desired.

WILD-WALNUT LEAVES

COLOR 83—*Light Tan*

2 pounds wild-walnut leaves
¼ cup raw alum
1 pound yarn

Boil the walnut leaves in 4 gallons of water for 1 or 2 hours. Strain. Add alum. Stir well and boil 10 minutes. Add the wet yarn and stir well. Boil 1 to 3 hours, depending upon depth of color desired. Rinse.

txohłitchii'

COLOR 84—*Salmon-Pink*

4   gallons very thick brick-colored rainwater from red mesas in New
    Mexico and Arizona

½   pound yarn

Dip up the water, which collects in puddles immediately following a heavy rain. Add wet yarn. Stir well. Boil for 4 hours, adding clear water to the dyebath as needed to keep sufficient liquid in the pot. Rinse.

The redder the clay used, the deeper will be the color of the yarn.

Red Dye for Moccasins

Inseparably connected in the minds of the Navajo with the dyeing of wool is the dyeing of buckskin ('abanih) for use as moccasins. A mordant and dye materials are also employed in the coloring of buckskin.

Juniper ashes

Mountain mahogany root bark

Alder bark

Tanned deerskin

Pick some branches of juniper and burn them to ashes and rub these ashes into the hair side of tanned deerskin, the hair having been previously removed in the process of tanning.

Boil the roots of the mountain mahogany ('esdaazih) and, while still lukewarm, sop the liquid on the ash-covered buckskin. Sprinkle dry ground-alder-bark powder prepared on a *metate* or Navajo grinding stone all over the surface of the buckskin, which has been wet with the mountain mahogany root dye. Fold the buckskin and allow to remain overnight so that the dye will bite in. In the morning the surface of the buckskin will be a red color.

Only one side of the buckskin is dyed, this side being the outside or hair side. It may be redyed from time to time as desired. The inside of the moccasins is undyed.